A **TRUE** BOOK™

The Cheyenne

**KEVIN CUNNINGHAM
AND PETER BENOIT**

Children's Press®
An Imprint of Scholastic Inc.
New York Toronto London Auckland Sydney
Mexico City New Delhi Hong Kong
Danbury, Connecticut

Content Consultant

Scott Manning Stevens, PhD
Director, McNickle Center
Newberry Library
Chicago, IL

Library of Congress Cataloging-in-Publication Data

Cunningham, Kevin, 1966–
 The Cheyenne/Kevin Cunningham and Peter Benoit.
   p. cm.—(A true book)
 Includes bibliographical references and index.
 ISBN-13: 978-0-531-20759-8 (lib. bdg.)   978-0-531-29301-0 (pbk.)
 ISBN-10: 0-531-20759-5 (lib. bdg.)   0-531-29301-7 (pbk.)
1. Cheyenne Indians—Juvenile literature. I. Benoit, Peter, 1955– II.Title.
 E99.C53C86 2011
 978.004'97353—dc22   2010049082

All rights reserved. Published in 2011 by Children's Press, an imprint of Scholastic Inc.
Printed in China 62
SCHOLASTIC, CHILDREN'S PRESS, A TRUE BOOK and associated logos are trademarks and/or registered trademarks of Scholastic Inc.

2 3 4 5 6 7 8 9 10 R 19 18 17 16 15 14 13 12

Find the Truth!

Everything you are about to read is true *except* for one of the sentences on this page.

Which one is **TRUE**?

T or F The Dog Soldiers wanted to make peace with American settlers.

T or F Bison provided the Cheyenne with food, tools, clothing, and shelter.

Find the answers in this book.

3

Contents

THE **BIG** TRUTH!

Peace pipe

3 Daily Life of the Cheyenne

How did the Cheyenne live?

4 Beliefs and Rituals

What did the Cheyenne believe in and
how did they show it?

5 Cheyenne Society

What was the Council of Forty-Four?

About 20,000 Cheyenne live
in the United States today.

5

This map shows where the Cheyenne lived prior to the 1800s and where their reservations are today.

Canada

Hudson Bay

Pacific Ocean

Montana

North Dakota

Minnesota

Wyoming

South Dakota

United States

Atlantic Ocean

Oklahoma

N
W   E
S

Gulf of Mexico

Mexico

LEGEND

Cheyenne lands before 1800s

Cheyenne migration

Cheyenne lands at time of Euorpean contact

Present-day Cheyenne Reservations

CHAPTER 1

War and Peace

The Cheyenne's histories told of their people being pushed from lands in the north by powerful enemies. They crossed great waters, the tales said, and settled in what is now Minnesota. The French explorer René-Robert Cavelier, Sieur de La Salle first described them in 1680 as peaceful fishers and farmers. They grew maize (corn), beans, and squash and lived in bark-covered wigwams. But their peaceful life was about to change.

Native peoples called maize, beans, and squash the Three Sisters.

Cheyenne means "red talkers" in the Sioux language.

The Move West

The Cree, an enemy of the Cheyenne, bought guns from French traders. Unable to fight their foes, the Cheyenne moved westward into today's North and South Dakota. There they learned of huge bison herds on the Great Plains. They also bought horses. The horses helped them hunt and become more mobile. Soon, another Plains people, the Sioux, bought guns for war. The Cheyenne moved again, into an area around Wyoming's North Platte River.

As the Cheyenne continued to **migrate**, three branches of their people became one. After a time, the Cheyenne split into 10 bands, or groups. Each had its own leaders. But **tradition** held the Cheyenne together. The Sun Dance was one religious practice that all Cheyenne shared. In times of war, the **Sacred** Arrow Ceremony and smoking the war pipe brought bands together to fight.

The Cheyenne sometimes smoked pipes as part of religious ceremonies or to seal agreements.

A New Way of Life

By the 1800s, the Cheyenne lived like other Plains Indians. They had given up farming to become **nomads** on horseback. They traded wigwams for teepees. These teepees could set up or take down in minutes. Bison meat and wild plants became important parts of their diet. They also fought ongoing wars with two Native American groups. One was a nomadic people known as the Crow. The other was the Pawnee Plains people who hunted and lived in villages.

Tepees were easy to put up and take down.

A Cheyenne village could be packed up in an hour.

10

The Santa Fe Trail ran from Franklin, Missouri, to Santa Fe, New Mexico.

The Santa Fe Trail opened in 1821, bringing white settlers west. Cheyenne horsemen started raiding the trail's travelers. The trail was important for carrying goods for trade. The U.S. Army also used it as a highway. Worried about raids, the U.S. government encouraged the Cheyenne to trade with travelers rather than attack them. The Cheyenne agreed, and the two sides signed a peace **treaty** in 1825.

More Settlers, More Trouble

By the 1840s, however, problems returned. More settlers pushed west in search of cheap land and gold. On the Plains, they competed with native peoples for buffalo and hard-to-find fresh water. Whites also brought new diseases. **Cholera**, an illness caused by bad water and human waste, followed traders across the Plains. In 1849, cholera killed more than half of the Cheyenne people in a single summer.

It took pioneers four to six months to travel to the West Coast.

In the 1840s, thousands of white settlers crossed the Great Plains every year.

12

Native Americans sometimes fought the white settlers who crossed their land.

A gold rush in 1849 brought even more travelers west. In 1851, the government agreed to recognize the territory of the Northern Cheyenne, the Arapaho, and other peoples. The land included half of today's Colorado and parts of Nebraska, Kansas, and Wyoming. The Cheyenne let the U.S. government build roads across their land in return for money and supplies. But whites continued to clash with the Cheyenne. The violence soon led to war.

U.S. soldiers often attacked
the Cheyenne people.

CHAPTER 2

War in the West

In 1856, a Cheyenne warrior was attacked on a bridge over the Platte River in Wyoming. Angered, his band swept down on three groups of travelers that summer. The U.S. Army rode out to punish the band. The soldiers killed about a dozen Cheyenne. The trouble worsened in 1859 when miners struck gold in what would become Colorado. Miners and settlers suddenly surged onto Cheyenne lands.

 The Cheyenne attacked on the Platte River Bridge had been fleeing arrest for stealing horses.

The Treaty of Fort Wise

In February 1861, the U.S. government offered a peace treaty to the Cheyenne at Fort Wise. The new treaty canceled out the 1851 deal that had recognized Cheyenne lands. Instead, the Cheyenne had to move to a small area in southeast Colorado. The area was one-thirteenth the size of their old territory. Cheyenne leader Black Kettle and some of his followers, wanting peace, signed the new treaty. Many other Cheyenne, however, refused.

In 1861, the Cheyenne people had to move because the U.S. government limited their territory.

When facing death, a Dog Soldier sang a sacred song.

Dog soldiers perform a dance.

Dog Soldiers

The Cheyenne had five warrior societies. They were known as the Fox, the Elk, the Shield, the Dog, and the Bowstring. Some of the fiercest Cheyenne belonged to the Dog Soldiers. They were the best of the best of the warriors. The Dog Soldiers believed in fighting the whites' movement onto their lands. In battle, they were fearless. A Dog Soldier used a sacred arrow to pin a piece of a special belt to the ground. From that moment on, he stood his ground against all enemies, or died.

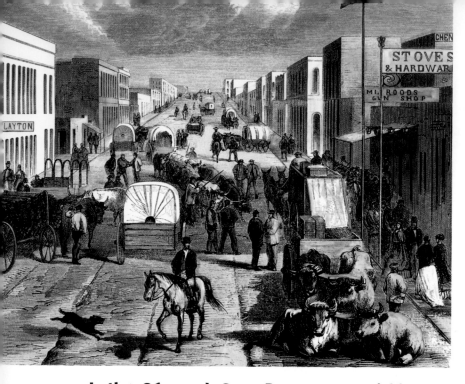

Denver was founded in 1858.

In the 1860s and 1870s, Denver grew quickly, increasing its need for space and supplies.

After the Fort Wise treaty, the Dog Soldiers left the rest of the Cheyenne. The warriors began to fight on their own against anyone moving west. Three years later, the governor of Colorado approved attacks on the Cheyenne. His decision ended all chances for peace. Warriors from several native groups soon raided the trail going into Denver, cutting off supplies to the city.

An Attempt at Peace

In November 1864, U.S. officials offered to talk with the Cheyenne and their allies. The peace meeting would be held at Sand Creek, Colorado. Black Kettle led about 800 people there. The army promised to protect Black Kettle's followers. The Native Americans showed up with the white flag of **truce**. Black Kettle also flew an American flag over his lodge to show his friendship with the United States. Then things went terribly wrong.

Native Americans discuss peace with U.S. soldiers.

Massacre at Sand Creek

Colonel John Chivington and his soldiers, wanting a fight, swept into Black Kettle's village. In the **massacre** that followed, about 130 Cheyenne were killed. More than 100 of them were women and children. The soldiers came back later and murdered those who had been injured in the first attack. Though Black Kettle escaped, several Cheyenne leaders—many of whom wanted peace—died in the Sand Creek Massacre.

Today, Sand Creek is a national historic site.

Seven hundred U.S. soldiers attacked an Indian camp in the Sand Creek Massacre.

Black Kettle

Black Kettle (back row, middle) was part of a Cheyenne deligation that sought peace with the U.S. government.

Black Kettle believed that the Cheyenne could not match the whites' numbers or power. Peace, he felt, was a better option than war. He continued to push for peace after the U.S. government broke its promises. He argued for peace even after nearly losing his wife at Sand Creek. In fact, when Black Kettle was killed in an attack a few years later, he was still flying a white flag over his teepee.

Custer died in a massive Indian
attack on June 25-26, 1876.

War

The Dog Soldiers
believed the massacre
made it clear that
peace would not work.
After Sand Creek, they
and warriors from the
Sioux and Arapaho raided
along the South Platte

**George A. Custer was a bold and
sometimes foolhardy soldier.**

River. The thousand-man
force attacked forts and
killed settlers, including women and children.
In 1868, the army sent in the **cavalry** under the
command of George A. Custer. Custer was to put
down the Indian threat once and for all.

Custer and his men attack the Cheyenne camp along the Washita River in what is now Oklahoma.

Custer's men entered Cheyenne lands at the Washita River. On November 27, 1868, Custer ordered an attack on the camp led by Black Kettle. Black Kettle died in the battle. An unknown number of Cheyenne and 21 army soldiers were also killed. In the years to come, fighting and disease continued to harm the Cheyenne. Though they held out into the 1870s, eventually the Cheyenne had to move onto **reservations** for good.

Medicine Wheel: A Sacred Place

Sometimes the Cheyenne built permanent structures for their religious practices. One of the best known is Big Horn Medicine Wheel. This ancient circle of stones sits 9,642 feet (2,939 meters) above sea level on Medicine Mountain near Lovell, Wyoming. Early versions of the wheel may have been built as long as 800 years ago. Big Horn is the southernmost medicine wheel. Many more exist in Canada.

Big Wheel

Big Horn Medicine Wheel is 80 feet (24.4 m) wide. That makes it one of the largest medicine wheels in North America.

Tracking the Days

Each of the 28 spokes inside the wheel represents a day of the lunar month. It takes the moon 28 days to go through all of its phases.

    Some experts think that medicine wheels were used to hold ceremonies celebrating a change of season. Certain spokes point toward where the sun rises on the first day of fall, winter, spring, and summer.

Bison were the main source of food and other supplies for Indians on the Plains.

CHAPTER 3

Daily Life of the Cheyenne

When the Cheyenne became hunters on horseback, they adopted the ways of other Plains peoples. One of the most important parts of Plains life was the bison, or the American buffalo. This huge animal could stand 6 feet 5 inches (200 centimeters) tall, weigh 1,800 pounds (800 kilograms) and more, and run 30 miles (50 kilometers) per hour. Millions of the plant-eating beasts roamed up and down the Plains.

← A hunter marked his arrows so he could find his own kills.

Bison can breed with cattle to make beefalos.

A bison's shaggy fur could be made into a warm robe.

All-Purpose Animal

The Cheyenne got about 800 pounds (350 kg) of meat from a large bull (male) bison. But they did more than eat the bison. The skin became clothes and covers for the teepees. Cheyenne craftsmen turned the horns into tools, knives, and spoons. A bison heart made a good bag. When the Cheyenne learned to use the bison so fully, they started following the herds. They packed and unpacked the teepees as they went.

Hunting, Horses, and Herds

Before the Cheyenne owned horses, they made V-shaped pens out of fallen trees and rocks. Bison were driven inside and killed. Methods changed after Europeans brought horses over from Europe. Horses allowed the Cheyenne to surround a bison herd and then shoot arrows for the kill. Most bison meat was dried in the sun. The dried meat was lightweight and could last a long time. It was easily carried and eaten on the march.

A Native American woman prepares a bison hide. It could be used to make clothing or teepees.

Bison for Sale

The Cheyenne hunted in summer. During the harsh Plains winters, they gathered together in villages and waited out the cold. They sat around fires, wearing warm clothes made from the skins of bison or deer. Later, however, the Cheyenne began to hunt bison to sell the skins to whites. More bison had to be hunted to meet the demand. Native American hunters were soon killing bison by the tens of thousands. Bison populations decreased dramatically.

Bent's Fort was the first major white settlement on the Santa Fe Trail.

Native Americans exchanged bison hides for pots, knives, fabric, and other goods at trading posts such as Bent's Fort in Colorado.

Men and Women

Cheyenne men hunted and made war. The women cooked, cared for children, made clothing, and set up and took down the teepee. When a man married, he went to live with his wife's band. The tradition changed, however, when the Dog Soldiers turned against the old ways. In their bands, the women came to live with the husband's people. As the conflicts with whites heated up, other Cheyenne began to accept the Dog Soldiers' ways.

Cheyenne women usually carried their children on their backs.

Young Cheyenne

Adults almost never punished the Cheyenne children and did not often need to. Girls and boys had different upbringings. Girls, for instance, learned how to cook bison, sew clothes, and set up the teepee. Boys, meanwhile, practiced hunting with their fathers and with other boys in the band. All children learned traditional stories from the elders around a campfire. These stories taught lessons and history, and also entertained listeners.

Cheyenne children often played with toys made from buffalo bones.

Cheyenne children sometimes wore elaborate costumes for ritual dances.

Plains Play

A favorite game among the Cheyenne and many Plains peoples was the hoop and pole game. A person made a hoop out of branches and wrapped it in bison skin. Inside he created a sort of net. As the hoop rolled along, players tried to throw a pole or shoot an arrow through holes in the net. Boys held games for fun and to practice with weapons. Men, however, played to win horses and other valuable goods.

The Sun Dance was performed in structures such as this one.

CHAPTER 4

Beliefs and Rituals

The Cheyenne religion included many **rituals**. One of the most important was the Sun Dance. The Sun Dance celebrated the birth of the universe. This included the planets, moon, and stars, as well as the animals of the earth. The Cheyenne often performed the Sun Dance in times of starvation. This is because their legends recalled an earlier time of starvation. In the legends, Maheo, the Great Spirit, eased their hunger by showing them the Sun Dance.

Sun Dancers believed a sacred hat they wore as they danced gave them control over animals.

Inside the Sweat Lodge

Some Cheyenne rituals took place in sweat lodges. These were built of bison skins wrapped around a dome of bent willow branches. A pit in the center of the lodge held glowing hot stones and special herbs. The temperature inside the lodge was so high that the men would sweat. The heat, with smoke from the herbs, caused a **hallucination**, or vision. The Cheyenne believed that it provided advice or wisdom. Men left the lodge "reborn," ready to face the important tasks of life.

Timeline of Cheyenne–U.S. Struggles

1825
The Cheyenne sign their first peace treaty with the United States.

1849
Cholera kills more than half the Cheyenne.

Sacred Objects

Cheyenne stories told of how the great Cheyenne leader Sweet Medicine received four sacred arrows. The two Buffalo Arrows, when pointed at a herd, confused the animals and made them easier to hunt. The two Man Arrows blinded the Cheyenne's enemies. Cheyenne bands kept copies of the four arrows and other objects in a guarded teepee. The people believed the sacred objects gave the Cheyenne power and linked them to their ancestors.

1863
The Cheyenne fight a war with U.S. soldiers in Colorado.

1864
U.S. soldiers kill peace-seeking Cheyenne in the Sand Creek Massacre.

Cheyenne chiefs wore feather headdresses.

CHAPTER 5

Cheyenne Society

Though the Cheyenne lived in 10 different bands, they sometimes acted as a single people. Four chiefs from each band plus four other respected chiefs formed the Council of Forty-Four. The council led the Cheyenne as a kind of **government**. They worked to keep peace among bands and discussed treaties and friendship with other peoples. In normal times, the council met once every four years.

A member of the Council of Forty-Four chose the man he wanted to replace him.

The Council of Forty-Four did not usually include warriors.

Military Societies

The council, however, did not control **military** matters or hunting. Instead, six special military societies made those decisions. The Dog Soldiers were one of the societies. Each society invited the bravest and most respected warriors to join. At times, a member of a military society was asked to join the council. When that happened, he had to leave the military society to serve as one of the forty-four.

Each military society took a turn deciding on war matters for the whole Cheyenne people. In peacetime, the societies kept order in the Cheyenne bands. But the system broke down when Dog Soldiers split from the other Cheyenne. As a result, the Dog Soldiers became their own band for many years.

Dog soldiers often wore breastplates made of bones.

Other Cheyenne military societies included the Swift Fox and the Elk Warriors.

Continuing History

Over the years, the Cheyenne were split into two groups. This happened through American settlement and conflicts with the U.S. government. Today, most Cheyenne in the north live on the Northern Cheyenne Reservation in Montana. Southern Cheyenne share a reservation with the Arapaho in Oklahoma. Each reservation has its own schools and government. Religious ceremonies are still performed, many of which are closed to outsiders. The Cheyenne language is also kept alive on these reservations. ★

Many Cheyenne people today take part in traditional dances.

True Statistics

Number of Cheyenne bands: 10

Length of the Sun Dance: 3-4 days

Percentage of Cheyenne killed by cholera in 1849: More than 50 percent

Number of Cheyenne at Sand Creek: Around 800

Width of Big Horn Medicine Wheel: 80 ft. (24.4 m)

Spikes in Big Horn Medicine Wheel: 28

Height of a large bison: 6 ft. 5 in. (200 cm)

Speed of a running bison: 30 mph (50 kph)

Amount of meat in a large bison: 800 lbs. (350 kg)

Number of men on the Cheyenne's council: 44

Width of a large sweat lodge: 20 ft. (6 m)

Number of sacred arrows kept by the Cheyenne: 4

Cheyenne population today: In 2000, 3,250 Northern Cheyenne lived in Montana, and in 2003, about 8,000 Southern Cheyenne lived in Oklahoma

Did you find the truth?

F The Dog Soldiers wanted to make peace with American settlers.

T Bison provided the Cheyenne with food, tools, clothing, and shelter.

Resources

Books

Birchfield, D. L. *Cheyenne*. New York: Gareth Stevens, 2003.

De Capua, Sarah. *The Cheyenne*. New York: Benchmark, 2006.

Englar, Mary. *The Cheyenne*. Mankato, MN: Capstone, 2000.

Hill, Rick, and Teri Frazier. *Indian Nations of North America*. Washington, DC: National Geographic, 2010.

Marrin, Albert. *Saving the Buffalo*. New York: Scholastic, 2006.

Miller, Jay. *American Indian Festivals*. New York: Children's Press, 1996.

Press, Petra. *The Cheyenne*. Minneapolis, MN: Compass Point, 2002.

Ryan, Marla Felkins, and Linda Schmittroth. *Cheyenne*. San Diego, CA: Blackbirch, 2002.

Somervill, Barbara A. *American Bison*. Ann Arbor, MI: Cherry Lake, 2007.

Organizations and Web Sites

Cheyenne and Arapaho Tribes of Oklahoma

www.c-a-tribes.org

Read about Cheyenne and Arapaho culture and learn about events taking place among the Southern Cheyenne.

Northern Cheyenne Tribe

www.cheyennenation.com

Find out what's happening today on the Northern Cheyenne Reservation in southeastern Montana.

Smithsonian Institution: Tichkematse

www.nmnh.si.edu/naa/squint_eyes/squint_eyes.htm

Learn the fascinating life story of a Cheyenne explorer and artist who also worked for the Smithsonian Institution.

Places to Visit

National Museum of the American Indian

Fourth Street & Independence Ave., SW
Washington, DC 20560
(202) 633-1000
www.nmai.si.edu
View exhibits about the lives and cultures of Native Americans.

Sand Creek Massacre National Historic Site

County Road W and County Road 54
Eads, CO 81036
www.nps.gov/sand
Visit the site of the tragic massacre of Cheyenne villagers.

Important Words

cavalry (KAV-uhl-ree)—soldiers mounted on horseback

cholera (KOL-ur-uh)—a deadly disease caused by bad water

government (GUHV-urn-muhnt)—the control and administration of a nation, state, or organization

hallucination (huh-loo-sun-NAY-shun)—a dreamlike vision

massacre (MASS-uh-kur)—the killing of helpless or peaceful people

migrate (MYE-grate)—to move from one place to another

military (MIL-uh-ter-ee)—relating to war

nomads (NOH-madz)—people who move from place to place

reservations (rez-ur-VAY-shuhnz)—land set aside for use by Native Americans

rituals (RICH-oo-ulz)—religious ceremonies with specific rules

sacred (SAY-krid)—having to do with religion or something holy

tradition (truh-DISH-uhn)—a pattern of thought or action passed down from generation to generation

treaty (TREE-tee)—an agreement or deal that is legally binding on the two or more groups that sign

truce (TROOSS)—an agreement to quit fighting

Index

Page numbers in **bold** indicate illustrations

47

About the Authors

Kevin Cunningham has written more than 40 books on disasters, the history of disease, Native Americans, and other topics. Cunningham lives near Chicago with his wife and young daughter.

Peter Benoit is educated as a mathematician but has many other interests. He has taught and tutored high school and college students for many years, mostly in math and science. He also runs summer workshops for writers and students of literature. Benoit has written more than 2,000 poems. His life has been one committed to learning. He lives in Greenwich, New York.